D1544773

American Lives

Kit
Carson

Rick Burke

Heinemann Library
Chicago, Illinois

© 2004 Heinemann Library
a division of Reed Elsevier Inc.
Chicago, Illinois

Customer Service 888-454-2279
Visit our website at www.heinemannlibrary.com

Designed by Sarah Figlio
Photo Research by Alan Gottlieb
Printed and Bound in the United States by
Lake Book Manufacturing, Inc.

08 07 06 05 04
10 9 8 7 6 5 4 3 2 1

**Library of Congress
Cataloging-in-Publication Data**
Burke, Rick, 1957-
   Kit Carson / by Rick Burke.
      v. cm. -- (American lives)
Includes bibliographical references (p.) and index.
Contents: Leader -- Childhood -- Saddles -- New
Mexico -- Taking back horses -- Trappers -- Fremont
-- Sierra Nevada Mountains -- Mexican War --
Meeting the president -- Indian agent -- Civil War --
Remembering Kit.
   ISBN 1-4034-4192-8 -- ISBN 1-4034-4200-2 (pbk.)
 1. Carson, Kit, 1809-1868--Juvenile literature. 2.
Pioneers--West (U.S.)--Biography--Juvenile
literature. 3. Frontier and pioneer life--West (U.S.)--
Juvenile literature. 4. Scouts and scouting--West
(U.S.)--Biography--Juvenile literature. 5. Soldiers--
West (U.S.)--Biography--Juvenile literature. 6. West
(U.S.)--Biography--Juvenile literature. 7. West
(U.S.)--History--To 1848--Juvenile literature. [1.
Carson, Kit, 1809-1868. 2. Pioneers. 3. Soldiers. 4.
Scouts and scouting. 5. West (U.S.)--History--19th
century.] I. Title. II. American lives (Heinemann
Library (Firm))
   F592.C33B87 2003
   978'.02'092--dc21

                                            2003004972

Acknowledgments
The author and publishers are grateful to the
following for permission to reproduce copyright
material: Title page Corbis; pp. 4, 8, 10, 18 General
Research Division, Astor Lenox and Tilden
Foundations, New York Public Library; p. 5
Christie's Images/Corbis; pp. 6, 20 Michael Maslan
Historic Photography/Corbis; pp. 7, 24, 28, 29 Taos
Historic Museums; pp. 9, 12 Library of Congress;
pp. 10, 11 Bettman/Corbis; p. 13 Reproduced from
A Pictographic History of the Oglala Sioux, by
Amos Bad Heart Bull, text by Helen H. Blish
©renewed 1995 by the University of Nebraska
Press; p. 14 Robert Holmes/Corbis; p. 15 American
Heritage Center, University of Wyoming; p. 16
Joslyn Art Museum, Omaha, Nebraska; p. 17 North
Wind Picture Archives; p. 19 Hulton-Deutsch
Collection/Corbis; p. 21 Courtesy Franklin D.
Roosevelt Library, Hyde Park, NY; p. 22L courtesy
Southwest Museum, Los Angeles, Photo #C1.18; p.
22R The Corcoran Gallery of Art/Corbis; p. 23
courtesy Museum of New Mexico, Neg. #7151; pp.
25, 26 Western History Collection/Denver Public
Library; p. 27 Library of Congress/Neg.#LC-
USZC2-3516

Cover photograph by Underwood &
Underwood/Corbis

The publisher would like to thank Michelle Rimsa
for her comments in the preparation of this book.

Every effort has been made to contact copyright
holders of any material reproduced in this book.
Any omissions will be rectified in subsequent
printings if notice is given to the publisher.

Some words are shown in bold, **like this.** You can
find out what they mean by looking in the glossary.

The image of Kit Carson that appears on the cover of
this book is from an engraving by N. Orr, circa 1877.

Contents

Leader

When settlers first arrived in America, they wanted land for their new homes. The land along the East coast quickly filled up. People decided to move west, but they were not sure where to go. They needed a guide to lead the way. One of the most important guides in the history of the United States was Kit Carson. People like Kit showed the settlers where to go so they would be safe.

Kit rode many horses during his travels. This picture shows his favorite horse, Apache.

4

Many of the places that Kit explored had never been seen before by settlers. It was Kit's job to take people there safely. Sometimes this was a hard thing to do.

It takes a brave person to be responsible for the lives of others. Kit was a brave man. Kit was good at hunting and following animals through the wilderness. Kit was a small boy in Missouri when he learned the skills he would use the rest of his life. His bravery and skill in the woods helped him and the people he was leading.

Childhood

Kit was born on December 24, 1809, in Madison County, Kentucky. His parents, Lindsey and Rebecca, named him Christopher, but they called him Kit. Kit was one of ten children Lindsey and Rebecca had together. When Kit was one year old, the Carson family moved to Missouri. Missouri had plenty of land and many animals to hunt.

Kentucky

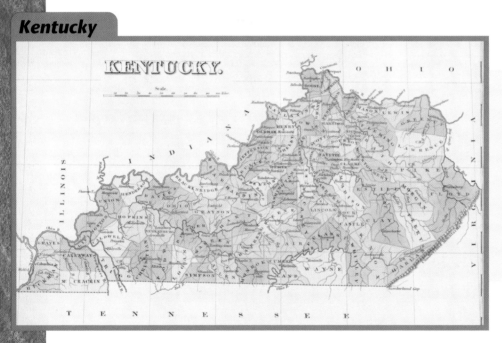

Kentucky had many settlers living there before people began to move west.

The Life of Kit Carson

1809	1821	1825	1831
Born on December 24 in Madison County, Kentucky	*Became an **apprentice** to a saddle maker*	*Ran away to New Mexico*	*Joined the Rocky Mountain Fur Company*

6

Kit Carson was born in the house shown above. His birthplace is now a **historic** site in Richmond, Kentucky.

When Kit was eight years old, there was a terrible accident. Kit's father was clearing land and burning wood. A large tree branch fell on him and killed him. From then on, Kit and his brother ran the farm. Kit hunted so his family could have food to eat.

1835	1843	1853	1868
Married Waanibe	*Joined John Frémont to look for the Buenaventura River*	*Became an Indian **agent***	*Died on May 23*

Saddles

When Kit was twelve years old, his mother married a man named Joseph Martin. When Kit was fifteen years old, he became an **apprentice** to David Workman. Workman was a saddle maker.

Saddle makers built saddles for horses. Many people moving west needed new saddles to make the journey.

Wanted: Runaway

When apprentices ran away, their bosses usually offered a reward for their return. David Workman wanted Kit to be happy, so he only offered a reward of one cent. He knew no one would capture Kit for that amount.

People went to Santa Fe because it was a center for trade. The Santa Fe Trail, which brought people from the east, ended there.

Workman was a nice man who treated Kit well, but Kit hated being inside a shop all day. He wanted to be outside, hunting. Travelers came to Workman's shop to buy new saddles and have their old saddles fixed. Kit loved to hear stories they told about New Mexico. New Mexico sounded like a place where he could be very happy. When he was sixteen, Kit ran away from Workman's shop.

New Mexico

Kit found a wagon train ready to leave for New Mexico. A wagon train was a group of people who traveled to a faraway place together. They hired Kit to take care of the animals and fix saddles on the trip.

Kit loved New Mexico. After two or three years, he found a job there as a fur trapper. A trapper caught animals and sold their fur for money.

Fur trappers in the 1800s used traps such as this Newhouse beaver trap to catch animals.

Kit learned how to trap beavers and other animals, find his way through mountains and land he had never seen, and stay away from people who wanted to steal his horse and furs. Kit sold the furs to traders for hundreds of dollars.

Traveling with a wagon trail took a long time. It could take several months to cross the United States.

Taking Back Horses

In 1831, Kit Carson joined the Rocky Mountain Fur Company. One night in 1833, while Carson and his group of trappers were asleep, 50 Crow warriors stole their horses. Carson and eleven other men followed the tracks of the **raiding** party. Carson's group found the Crow the next night. They crawled through the snow in the dark of the night and watched the Crow. The warriors were dancing around the campfire, happy about having stolen the horses.

Trappers and **frontiersmen** often met Native Americans during their travels. Many times, these meetings were not good. The Crow were known to be fierce fighters.

Native Americans stole from each other, too. The note at the top of this picture means "stealing at night" in the language of the Lakota.

Carson's group waited until the Crow went to sleep. The men then crawled over and untied the horses. To get the horses to move away from the camp without making any noise, the men threw snowballs at them. When the horses were safely away, the men attacked the sleeping Native Americans. They killed nearly every one of the Crow warriors.

The Importance of Horses

In some tribes, like the Crow, stealing horses from others was important. Horses could be traded for other things. In some tribes, boys were thought of as men after having stolen the horses of other tribes.

Trappers

Being a trapper was not easy work. The fur that trappers wanted most was beaver fur. Beaver fur was used to make expensive hats for men in cities in the United States and in Europe. The best time of year to get beaver fur was in winter, when beavers grew extra fur to keep themselves warm. Beavers built their homes in streams and ponds, so trappers set their traps near water.

Some people think that over 10,000 beavers were hunted each year to make the beaver skin hats.

The Mountain Man **Rendezvous** took place in Wyoming every summer. The trappers came together to sell furs, have contests, and tell stories.

Besides checking the traps every day for beavers, Carson's job was to hunt for meat for the men in the Rocky Mountain Fur Company. Carson was a very good hunter.

When summer came, trappers would stop their work and take their furs to a meeting place with traders near the mountains. Trappers would sell or trade their furs to the traders for money and goods.

Frémont

In the summer of 1835, Carson brought his furs to sell to traders. There he met a pretty Arapaho woman named Waanibe. Her name meant "Singing Grass." They fell in love and were married. Waanibe soon had a baby girl, Adaline. A year later, Waanibe gave birth to a second daughter. Both Waanibe and the baby

This famous painting is called *The Trapper's Bride*. It represents an American Fur Company trapper taking a wife.

died soon after. Carson tried to take care of Adaline, but it was too difficult in winter trapping camps. He took Adaline to St. Louis, Missouri, to be raised by his sister. In 1843, Carson married a woman named Josefa Jaramilla. They had several children together.

Carson met a man who would make him famous. The man was a **lieutenant** in the U.S. Army named John Frémont. He wanted to explore the land around the Rocky Mountains. Frémont hired Carson to guide him through the mountains. Carson and Frémont went on three journeys together. They became famous when stories of their adventures appeared in newspapers and books.

Traveling through the wilderness was often dangerous. There usually was not a path to take, and nothing to guide the way. Kit had to rely on his skills to survive.

Sierra Nevada Mountains

In 1843, Carson and Frémont hoped to find the Buenaventura—a river that was thought to flow from the Sierra Nevada Mountains. Carson and Frémont discovered that there was not a river like that. By the time they figured it out, it was winter. Carson's group could not go back the way they came because the trail was blocked by snow. If they stayed where they were, they would starve. However, if they continued to travel west, their lives were in danger as well.

The men in Carson and Frémont's group made camp by packing down snow. They used this area as a place to sleep for the night.

Traveling in an area like this is difficult. The men had to lead horses that were carrying a lot of supplies.

Despite the snowy conditions, they decided to head to the Sacramento Valley in California. The men had to pack the snow down with large hammers so they could walk on it. They had to break the ice that covered streams so they could drink. When a mule died, the group of men cooked and ate it.

Carson did not need maps or charts to find his way. If he saw a mountain pass or stream, he remembered it. Finally, Carson saw a mountain he had seen before. He led the group through a mountain pass to safety.

19

Mexican War

In 1846, the land that is now California was part of the country of Mexico. Some people wanted to separate California from Mexico so it could become part of the United States. Frémont and Carson joined a group of 428 men, called the California Battalion, to fight for California's freedom from Mexico. Frémont sent Carson to Washington, D.C., with a message. On his way, Carson met General Stephen Kearny. Kearny ordered Carson to lead him to California. Carson refused at first, saying that he was following an order from Frémont. However, Kearny was a higher-ranking officer than Frémont, so Carson had to obey him.

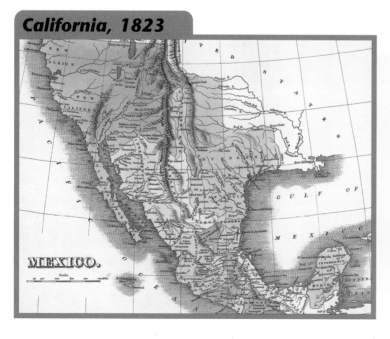

California, 1823

The people of the United States fought many battles with Mexico before getting the western land they wanted.

The Californios put up fierce fights to save their land. However, there were too many people fighting against them, and the United States claimed the land.

On December 6, 1846, Carson and Kearny's men were attacked by **Californios.** Many were killed or wounded. After two days of being attacked, Carson and two men slipped away to get help. They ran for 35 miles (56 kilometers) with no shoes on so they could not be followed. When they reached San Diego, they learned that help was on the way.

Meeting the President

A little over a month later, the war in California was over. The Mexican forces **surrendered** and a peace **treaty** was signed. The army needed to send news back to Washington, D.C., to let the leaders of the country know what happened. Carson was chosen to go. He arrived in Washington, D.C., in June 1847. Because of his trips with Frémont, Carson was famous. Men and women stopped Carson on the streets so they could meet him.

Jessie Benton Frémont

President James Polk

Carson never actually became a lieutenant in the United States Army. The U.S. **Senate** turned down Polk's request.

Another person who wanted to meet Kit was James Polk, the president of the United States. Frémont's wife, Jessie, took Kit to the White House. President Polk liked Kit. He made Kit a second **lieutenant** in the U.S. Army.

Statehood

California became the 31st state of the United States on September 9, 1850.

Indian Agent

More and more people were moving to the western area of the United States. They took the land of the native tribes that lived there. The government moved some tribes to places called **reservations.** Native Americans were not allowed to leave the reservations to hunt or to travel. Men in charge of reservations were called Indian **agents.** In 1853, Carson became an Indian agent for several of the tribes in northern New Mexico.

Carson is dressed in traditional Native American clothing. He is wearing a coat with fringe and fur, a vest, leggings, and moccasins.

Native Americans were not happy to be forced to live on reservations. They felt they should be able to live wherever they wanted, just like the settlers.

Some Indian agents were not honest. They stole the money that was supposed to be used to feed the Native Americans on the reservation. Carson was an honest man. He wrote many letters to Washington, D.C., to get money to feed the Native Americans under his control. Carson even spent his own money on food so they would not starve.

Civil War

In 1861, the Civil War started. This was a war between the northern and southern states. Eleven southern states wanted to form their own country called the Confederate States of America. The northern states, called the Union, fought to keep the United States together. Carson joined the New Mexico Volunteers to fight for the Union. He was given the rank of **lieutenant colonel.** Early in the war, soldiers were sent east to fight. Carson was given the job of protecting settlers from Native American **raids.**

Satanta was the war chief who led the Comanche against Carson and the New Mexico Volunteers.

Native Americans were always watching for anyone coming onto their land.

The U.S. government thought the Navajo living in New Mexico and Arizona were getting out of control. In 1863, Carson was sent there to force 8,000 Navajos to walk to their new **reservation** in New Mexico. This was called the Long Walk, and it was terrible for the Navajo. Carson and his men led the Native Americans along the 300-mile (483-kilometer) walk to the reservation. Many Navajo died, and those who survived lived in a prison-like camp for four years. To this day, the Navajo still feel hatred toward Kit.

Remembering Carson

The Civil War ended in April 1865. By then, Carson was a **brigadier general** in the army. The army sent him to be in charge of **Fort** Garland. Carson was getting old and he was in pain. He had a hard time breathing, but he still worried about others. He told **Congress** that the government was not doing enough to help the Native Americans. He said no one should be treated that poorly. Carson died on May 23, 1868. He had started to bleed **internally.**

Kit Carson is remembered as or of the greatest **frontiersmen** to ever live.

Namesakes

Carson City, Nevada, and Carson, Colorado, are named after Kit. Carson City is the state capital of Nevada. A state park in Taos, New Mexico, is also named for Carson.

This statue of Kit Carson is at Kit Carson State Park in Trinidad, Colorado.

Kit Carson was a brave man. Throughout his life, he saved the lives of others by using his knowledge and sometimes risking his own life. People counted on Carson. When life offered him different choices, he was not afraid to try them. Kit became good at many things in his life because he tried his best at whatever he did.

Glossary

agent person who acts or does business for another

apprentice person who is learning a trade or art by experience under a skilled worker

brigadier general officer in the army who is higher ranked than a lieutenant colonel

Californio Spanish-speaking people who had come from Mexico or Spain to settle in California

Congress part of U.S. government that makes laws

fort strong building used for defense against enemy attack

frontiersman person who explores unsettled areas, particularly in the United States

historic famous in history

internally happening inside the body

lieutenant officer in the army

lieutenant colonel officer in the army who is higher ranked than a lieutenant

raid attack

rendezvous planned meeting

reservation land set aside for use by Indian tribes

Senate part of the U.S. government

surrender give oneself to someone else of higher power

treaty agreement between two or more parties

More Books to Read

Boraas, Tracey. *Kit Carson, Mountain Man*. Mankato, Minn.: Capstone Press, Incorporated, 2002.

Ellis, Edward S., et al. *The Life of Kit Carson*. Fort Collins, Colo.: Lost Classics Book Company, 1998.

Glass, Andrew. *A Right Fine Life*. New York: Holiday House, 1997.

Mason, Augustus Lynch. *Indian Wars and Famous Frontiersmen*. Miami, Fla.: Fredonia Books, 2002.

Places to Visit

Kit Carson Home and Museum
Taos, New Mexico
Visitor Information: (505) 758-0505

Kit Carson Trail
Carson City, Nevada
Visitor Information: (775) 687-7410

Kit Carson Historical Society
Carson, Colorado
Visitor Information: (719) 962-3306

Index